ⓘBaker's®
Easy
CUT-UP
PARTY CAKES

PUBLICATIONS INTERNATIONAL, LTD.

FAVORITE ALL TIME RECIPES is a trademark of Publications International, Ltd.

BAKER'S, ANGEL FLAKE, GERMAN'S, ONE BOWL, DREAM WHIP, COOL WHIP and CALUMET are trademarks of Kraft General Foods, Inc., Glenview, Illinois 60025.

Photography by Sacco Productions Limited/Chicago
Illustrations by Rowena J. Vargas

Pictured on front cover *(clockwise from top right)*: Choochoo Train *(page 80)*, Play Ball *(page 64)* and Mr. Rabbit *(page 40)*.

Pictured on back cover *(clockwise from top left)*: Rollin' Fun *(page 66)*, Spot the Dog *(page 60)*, Baby Booties *(page 92)* and Old Glory *(page 20)*.

ISBN: 0-7853-0197-6

This edition published by Publications International, Ltd., 7373 North Cicero Avenue, Lincolnwood, Illinois 60646.

8 7 6 5 4 3 2 1

High Altitude Directions: Some recipes in this book may need to be adjusted for high altitude preparation. Call our toll-free number 9:00 a.m. to 4:00 p.m. (EST) weekdays (Continental U.S.) for information: 1-800-431-1001.

CONTENTS

Merry Christmas Tree (*page 38*)

Wacky Quacky Duck (*page 54*)

Umbrella (*page 94*)

CUT-UP CAKE BASICS

Cut-up cakes have long been a favorite dessert for parties and special occasions. These edible centerpieces are fun for adults as well as children to make and eat. BAKER'S Chocolates and BAKER'S ANGEL FLAKE Coconut are pleased to present a new book of the most requested classics as well as some brand new shapes for you to try.

All of the cakes can easily be made using one of the easy cake recipes that follow—or use a cake mix for even quicker results. Even if you aren't a confident cake decorator, there's no need to worry because BAKER'S ANGEL FLAKE Coconut will make you look like a pro.

Children love to help decorate cut-up cakes with coconut and candies and of course they love to eat them too! It is a great activity to share with them. But, cut-up cakes are not just for kids, so we have included recipes for all sorts of occasions and holidays. Bake cut-up cakes for birthdays, the Fourth of July, Halloween, the holiday season or just for fun. For instance, if you are having a shower, our Umbrella (page 94) or our Baby Booties (page 92) could be just the delicious centerpiece that adds a special touch to your party. And no one but you will know how easy these beautiful cakes are to make.

After paging through this publication, we know that you'll never look at cakes in the same way again and that you'll soon be able to add your own creative touches to any cake that you make.

CUT-UP CAKE TIPS

BEFORE YOU DECORATE

• Bake the cake the day before you plan to cut and decorate it if possible. A freshly baked cake can be difficult to work with as it may be too tender. If you don't have time to bake the cake the day ahead, place the cooled cake in the freezer for 30 to 45 minutes before cutting and decorating. Freezing the cake before cutting allows you to get the cleanest edges and least amount of crumbs.

• Cut the cakes using a long serrated knife in a sawing motion for the best results.

• Slice the rounded top off of your cake so that it is flat. If your cake is relatively flat, invert the cake and frost the flatter base of the cake.

• Brush off all of the loose cake crumbs with a soft pastry brush or gently with your hand before you begin to frost.

- Frost the cake with a long, flexible metal spatula for a smoother surface.

- Seal in the crumbs by first frosting the cake's cut edges with a thin layer of frosting. Let set for a few minutes. Clean crumbs off your spatula and frost the entire cake.

HOW TO STORE AND FREEZE CAKE LAYERS

- You can bake cakes up to one month before cutting and decorating so you always have a cake ready to cut up, assemble and decorate. To keep them moist, seal cooled cake(s) in an airtight freezer bag or wrap in heavy-duty aluminum foil. To protect your cakes in a crowded freezer, freeze wrapped cakes in the pans in which they were baked or in boxes. To thaw, let the wrapped frozen cakes stand at room temperature 1 hour for layers or 30 minutes for cupcakes.

- Do not store baked cakes made from cake mix in the refrigerator as they may become sticky and difficult to handle.

OTHER SHAPES

Standard cake pans are used for most of the cakes in this book: 8- or 9-inch round and square baking pans, 13 × 9-inch rectangular baking pans, 12-cup fluted tube pans, 9 × 5-inch loaf pans or 12-cup muffin pans. After the cakes are baked, cut them into pieces and arrange to make the desired shape. For rounded or dome-shaped cakes, use ovenproof glass bowls and custard cups. The recipe will specify the size. Check the size of a bowl by measuring how many cups of water it holds. Ovenproof glassware is available at many supermarkets and in stores that carry housewares.

SERVING PERFECT CAKES

- Keep your serving tray clean by tucking strips of waxed paper under the edges of the assembled cake pieces before frosting and applying coconut. When you are finished decorating the cake, gently slide the pieces of waxed paper out from under the cake. Add any decorations that are placed around the base of the cake after you remove the waxed paper.

- We've given suggestions for some ways to decorate the cakes, but don't be afraid to create your own designs.

EASY-STEP METHOD TO MAKE CUT-UP CAKES

Read before you start.

1. Select the cut-up cake you want to make.

2. Select a cake recipe (pages 6 to 11).

3. Using the chart following the cake recipe selected, find the pan sizes needed to make the cake you selected.

4. Read across the chart to find the amount of batter needed for each pan, oven temperature and baking times.

CAKE RECIPES

Following are three delicious recipes for cakes. You can also use cake mixes.

HEAVENLY WHITE CAKE

This cake is great when you want to tint the cake batter to complement the color of the coconut or frosting.

2⅓ cups flour
  2 teaspoons CALUMET Baking Powder
  ½ teaspoon salt
  4 egg whites

1½ cups sugar, divided
  ¾ cup shortening, margarine or butter
  1 cup milk
  1½ teaspoons vanilla

HEAT oven. See chart for specific temperature.

MIX flour, baking powder and salt; set aside.

BEAT egg whites until foamy. Gradually add ½ cup of the sugar, beating until soft peaks form; set aside.

BEAT shortening and remaining 1 cup sugar until light and fluffy. Beat in flour mixture alternately with milk until well blended and smooth. Mix in vanilla. With electric mixer on low speed, fold in egg whites. (Or fold in by hand.) Pour into greased and floured pans. Bake as directed in chart or until toothpick inserted in center comes out clean. Cool 10 minutes; remove from pans. Cool completely on wire racks.

HEAVENLY WHITE CAKE

PAN AND BOWL SIZE(S)	BATTER AMOUNT	OVEN TEMP	BAKE TIME
13 × 9-inch pan	all	350°	35 to 40 minutes
9-inch square baking pan	all	325°	55 to 60 minutes
two 8-inch baking pans (square or round)	half of batter in each pan	325°	35 to 40 minutes
two 9-inch baking pans (square or round)	half of batter in each pan	350°	30 to 35 minutes
9-inch square baking pan AND 8-inch round baking pan	half of batter in each pan	325°	35 to 40 minutes
1½-quart ovenproof glass bowl 1-quart ovenproof glass bowl 6-ounce custard cup	3¼ cups 1¾ cups ½ cup	325°	50 to 55 minutes 35 to 40 minutes 25 to 30 minutes
1½-quart ovenproof glass bowl 8-inch round baking pan 6-ounce custard cups	3 cups 2 cups ¼ cup	325°	50 to 55 minutes 30 to 35 minutes 15 to 20 minutes
1½-quart ovenproof glass bowl about 8 cupcakes	3 cups about ⅓ cup batter in each cup	325°	50 to 55 minutes 25 to 30 minutes
6-ounce custard cup two 9-inch round baking pans	¼ cup half of remaining batter in each pan	325°	20 to 25 minutes 35 to 40 minutes
about 24 cupcakes	about ⅓ cup batter in each cup	325°	25 to 30 minutes
two 9 × 5-inch loaf pans	half of batter in each pan	325°	30 to 35 minutes
12-cup fluted tube pan	all	325°	45 to 50 minutes

GERMAN SWEET CHOCOLATE SNACK CAKE

1 package (4 ounces) BAKER'S
    GERMAN'S Sweet
    Chocolate
3/4 cup (1 1/2 sticks) margarine or
    butter
1 1/2 cups sugar

3 eggs
1 teaspoon vanilla
2 cups flour, divided
1 teaspoon baking soda
1/4 teaspoon salt
1 cup buttermilk

HEAT oven. See chart for specific temperature.

MICROWAVE chocolate and margarine in large microwavable bowl on HIGH 2 minutes or until margarine is melted. **Stir until chocolate is completely melted.***

STIR sugar into chocolate mixture until well blended. With electric mixer on low speed, beat in eggs, one at a time, until completely mixed. Add vanilla.

BEAT in 1/2 cup flour, baking soda and salt. Beat in remaining 1 1/2 cups flour alternately with buttermilk until well blended and smooth. Pour into greased and floured pans. Bake as directed in chart until toothpick inserted in center comes out clean. Cool 10 minutes; remove from pans. Cool completely on wire racks.

*****Saucepan Preparation:** Melt chocolate and margarine in 3-quart saucepan on very low heat; stir constantly until just melted. Remove from heat.*

GERMAN SWEET CHOCOLATE SNACK CAKE

PAN AND BOWL SIZE(S)	BATTER AMOUNT	OVEN TEMP	BAKE TIME
13 × 9-inch pan	all	350°	50 to 55 minutes
9-inch square baking pan	all	325°	55 to 60 minutes
two 8-inch baking pans (square or round)	half of batter in each pan	350°	30 to 35 minutes
two 9-inch baking pans (square or round)	half of batter in each pan	350°	30 to 35 minutes
9-inch square baking pan AND 8-inch round baking pan	half of batter in each pan	325°	35 to 40 minutes
1½-quart ovenproof glass bowl 1-quart ovenproof glass bowl 6-ounce custard cup	2½ cups 1¾ cups ½ cup	325°	50 to 55 minutes 50 to 55 minutes 25 to 30 minutes
1½-quart ovenproof glass bowl 8-inch round baking pan 6-ounce custard cup	2½ cups 2¼ cups ¼ cup	325°	50 to 55 minutes 25 to 30 minutes 15 to 20 minutes
1½-quart ovenproof glass bowl about 8 cupcakes	2½ cups ⅓ cup batter in each cup	325°	45 to 50 minutes 25 to 30 minutes
6-ounce custard cup two 9-inch round baking pans	¼ cup half of remaining batter in each pan	325°	15 to 20 minutes 35 to 40 minutes
about 24 cupcakes	⅓ cup batter in each cup	325°	25 to 30 minutes
two 9 × 5-inch loaf pans	half of batter in each pan	325°	40 to 45 minutes
12-cup fluted tube pan	all	325°	50 to 55 minutes

BAKER'S ONE BOWL Chocolate CHOCOLATE CAKE

Try the easy One Bowl method used in this recipe the next time you are looking for a very chocolatey homemade cake.

6 squares BAKER'S Semi-Sweet Chocolate
³/₄ cup (1½ sticks) margarine or butter
1½ cups sugar
3 eggs

2 teaspoons vanilla
2½ cups flour, divided
1 teaspoon baking soda
¼ teaspoon salt
1½ cups water

HEAT oven. See chart for specific temperature.

MICROWAVE chocolate and margarine in large microwavable bowl on HIGH 2 minutes or until margarine is melted. **Stir until chocolate is completely melted.***

STIR sugar into melted chocolate mixture until well blended. With electric mixer on low speed, beat in eggs, one at a time, until completely mixed. Add vanilla.

STIR in ½ cup flour, baking soda and salt. Beat in remaining 2 cups flour alternately with water until well blended and smooth. Pour into greased and floured pans. Bake as directed in chart until toothpick inserted in center comes out clean. Cool 10 minutes; remove from pans. Cool completely on wire racks.

***Saucepan Preparation:** Melt chocolate and margarine in 3-quart saucepan on very low heat; stir constantly until just melted. Remove from heat.*

BAKER'S ONE BOWL CHOCOLATE CAKE

PAN AND BOWL SIZE(S)	BATTER AMOUNT	OVEN TEMP	BAKE TIME
13 × 9-inch pan	all	350°	55 to 60 minutes
9-inch square baking pan	all	325°	65 to 70 minutes
two 8-inch baking pans (square or round)	half of batter in each pan	325°	40 to 45 minutes
two 9-inch baking pans (square or round)	half of batter in each pan	350°	35 to 40 minutes
9-inch square baking pan AND 8-inch round baking pan	half of batter in each pan	350°	35 to 40 minutes
1½-quart ovenproof glass bowl 1-quart ovenproof glass bowl 6-ounce custard cup	3 cups 2¼ cups ½ cup	325°	50 to 55 minutes 45 to 50 minutes 25 to 30 minutes
1½-quart ovenproof glass bowl 8-inch round baking pan 6-ounce custard cup	3 cups 2¾ cups ¼ cup	325°	50 to 55 minutes 35 to 40 minutes 20 to 25 minutes
1½-quart ovenproof glass bowl about 12 cupcakes	3 cups about ⅓ cup batter in each cup	325°	50 to 55 minutes 20 to 25 minutes
6-ounce custard cup two 9-inch round baking pans	¼ cup half of remaining batter in each pan	325°	20 to 25 minutes 35 to 40 minutes
about 24 cupcakes	about ⅓ cup batter in each cup	350°	20 minutes
two 9x5-inch loaf pans	half of batter in each pan	325°	50 to 55 minutes
12-cup fluted tube pan	all	325°	55 to 60 minutes

FACTS ON FROSTING

MAKING PERFECT FROSTING

For frosting with a smooth velvety texture make sure that the margarine or butter is soft enough to cream with the other ingredients. Let margarine or butter stand at room temperature until softened but still cool. Margarine or butter that is too soft or melted will result in a frosting that doesn't have a creamy texture.

HOW TO TINT FROSTING

Add liquid food coloring one drop at a time to white frosting, mixing well after each drop. A little bit will go a long way so completely mix in one drop before adding another. For even more intense colors, use paste food coloring. It can be found in baking and kitchen specialty stores.

FROSTING RECIPES

Following are four great frosting recipes that are perfect for decorating any cake. COOL WHIP Whipped Topping or DREAM WHIP Whipped Topping Mix also make an easy frosting. You can also use store-bought frosting.

BAKER'S ONE BOWL
Chocolate
CHOCOLATE FROSTING

ONE BOWL
RECIPE ™

6 squares BAKER'S Semi-Sweet
    Chocolate
1 package (16 ounces)
    powdered sugar
    (about 4 cups)

⅓ cup milk
2 teaspoons vanilla
½ cup (1 stick) margarine or
    butter, softened, divided

MICROWAVE chocolate in large microwavable bowl on HIGH 2 minutes until chocolate is almost melted, stirring after each minute. **Stir until chocolate is completely melted.***

BEAT in sugar, milk, vanilla and 2 tablespoons margarine with electric mixer on low speed until well blended. Beat in remaining margarine until smooth. If frosting becomes too thick, beat in additional milk by teaspoonfuls until of spreading consistency.

Makes about 3 cups

***Saucepan Preparation:** Melt chocolate in 3-quart saucepan on very low heat; stir constantly until just melted. Remove from heat.*

VANILLA BUTTERCREAM FROSTING

1 package (16 ounces) powdered sugar (about 4 cups)

½ cup (1 stick) margarine or butter, softened
3 tablespoons milk
2 teaspoons vanilla

BEAT sugar, margarine, milk and vanilla with electric mixer on low speed until well blended and smooth. If frosting becomes too thick, beat in additional milk by teaspoonfuls until of spreading consistency.

Makes about 2½ cups

COCONUT-PECAN FROSTING

1½ cups (12-ounce can) evaporated milk
1½ cups sugar
4 egg yolks, slightly beaten
¾ cup (1½ sticks) margarine or butter, softened

1½ teaspoons vanilla
2 cups BAKER'S ANGEL FLAKE Coconut
1½ cups chopped pecans

MIX milk, sugar, egg yolks, margarine and vanilla in large saucepan.

COOK and stir on medium heat until mixture thickens and is golden, about 12 minutes. Remove from heat. Stir in coconut and pecans. Cool until thick enough to spread, stirring occasionally.

Makes about 4¼ cups

SEVEN MINUTE FROSTING

1½ cups sugar
½ cup water
2 egg whites

1 tablespoon light corn syrup
Dash of salt
1 teaspoon vanilla

MIX sugar, water, egg whites, corn syrup and salt in top of double boiler.

BEAT about 1 minute to blend thoroughly. Place over boiling water. Beat constantly with electric mixer on high speed until frosting stands in stiff peaks, about 7 minutes, scraping sides occasionally with rubber scraper.

REMOVE from boiling water. Immediately pour into large bowl. Add vanilla; beat until thick enough to spread, about 1 minute.

Makes about 5⅓ cups

WHIPPED TOPPINGS

COOL WHIP Whipped Toppings come in four different sizes of containers. To estimate your recipe needs, the content amounts are:

Container	COOL WHIP Amount	COOL WHIP Extra Creamy Amount	COOL WHIP Lite Amount
4 ounces	1¾ cups		
8 ounces	3½ cups	3 cups	3¼ cups
12 ounces	5¼ cups	4½ cups	5 cups
16 ounces	7 cups		

DREAM WHIP Whipped Topping Mix makes about 2 cups per envelope. It can be used in the recipes which call for COOL WHIP. To tint whipped topping, gently stir or fold food coloring into amount of whipped topping called for in selected recipe.

Cakes frosted with whipped toppings should be stored in the refrigerator.

GUMDROP GARNISHES

GUMDROP SHAPES

GUMDROP RIBBON

1. Flatten gumdrops with rolling pin on a smooth flat surface or sheet of waxed paper sprinkled with sugar. Roll until very thin (about ¹/₁₆-inch thick), turning frequently to coat with sugar. Cut into desired shapes.

1. Line up gumdrops in a row on a smooth flat surface or a sheet of waxed paper sprinkled with sugar. Flatten into long strips with a rolling pin, turning it frequently to coat with sugar.

2. Cut flattened gumdrops into a strip as needed.

NOTE: If you can't find large gumdrops, simply press several small gumdrops together before flattening with the rolling pin. Chewy fruit snack rolls can also be used for cutting out shapes.

COCONUT TIPS

BAKER'S ANGEL FLAKE Coconut is especially produced and packaged to be the moistest coconut possible and will ensure moister cakes and desserts. BAKER'S ANGEL FLAKE Coconut comes in several convenient package sizes:

- Each 14-ounce bag contains $5\frac{1}{3}$ cups of loosely packed coconut.

- Each 7-ounce bag or can contains about $2\frac{2}{3}$ cups of loosely packed coconut.

TO STORE COCONUT

Unopened packages of BAKER'S ANGEL FLAKE Coconut can be kept on your kitchen shelf. After opening the package, store it in the refrigerator in a tightly reclosed package or in an airtight container.

TO TOAST COCONUT

Heat oven to 350°F. Spread BAKER'S ANGEL FLAKE Coconut in an even layer in a shallow baking pan. Toast 7 to 12 minutes or until lightly browned. Stir the coconut or shake the pan frequently so that it will brown evenly. Or, toast in microwave oven on HIGH, 5 minutes for $1\frac{1}{3}$ cups coconut, stirring several times.

TO TINT COCONUT

Place 1 cup BAKER'S ANGEL FLAKE Coconut in a plastic bag. Dilute a few drops of food coloring with $\frac{1}{2}$ teaspoon water and add to coconut. Close the bag securely and shake until the coconut is evenly tinted. Repeat with more food coloring and water for a darker shade, if desired. For more intense colors, use paste food coloring mixed with water. It can be found at baking and kitchen specialty stores.

TO MAKE CHOCOLATE-COATED COCONUT

MICROWAVE 2 squares BAKER'S Semi-Sweet Chocolate in microwavable bowl on HIGH 1 to 2 minutes until almost melted, stirring every 30 seconds. **Stir until completely melted**. Add $1\frac{1}{3}$ cups BAKER'S ANGEL FLAKE Coconut; mix well. Spread onto cookie sheet, separating flakes of coconut with a fork. Use a toothpick to separate clumps. Refrigerate until chocolate is set. Store in tightly covered jar. Makes about $1\frac{1}{2}$ cups.

Sweet Heart

1²/₃ cups Vanilla Buttercream
    Frosting (page 13)
Red food coloring
1¹/₃ cups BAKER'S ANGEL
    FLAKE Coconut
1 (8-inch) square cake, cooled*
1 (8-inch) round cake layer,
    cooled*
2 large red gumdrops
    (for hearts)
1 large white gumdrop
    (for heart)
Chewy fruit snack roll (cut
    into strips for bow)

*Divide batter evenly between
8-inch square and 8-inch round
baking pans. Bake as directed in
chart for selected cake recipe.*

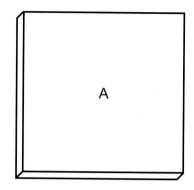

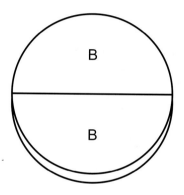

1. Tint frosting pink using red food coloring (see page 12 for directions). Tint coconut pink using red food coloring (see page 15 for directions).

2. Leave square cake whole; cut round cake in half as shown in illustration.

3. Using small amount of frosting to hold pieces together, arrange cake on serving tray as shown in photograph.

4. Frost cake with remaining frosting. Sprinkle with coconut.

5. Flatten gumdrops with rolling pin (see page 14 for directions); cut into 2-inch heart shapes with a small cookie cutter or sharp knife. Decorate cake with heart cut-outs and bow as shown in photograph.

Makes 12 to 16 servings

Lucky Shamrock

2²/₃ cups BAKER'S ANGEL FLAKE Coconut
Green food coloring
3 (9-inch) round cake layers, cooled*
1²/₃ cups Vanilla Buttercream Frosting (page 13)
2 large green gumdrops (for shamrocks)
1 large white gumdrop (for shamrocks)
Green decorating icing (for piping on cake)
Green decorating gel (for piping on shamrocks)

* Prepare and bake selected cake recipe two times using 9-inch round baking pans. Use three of the layers for cake. Reserve remaining layer for another use.

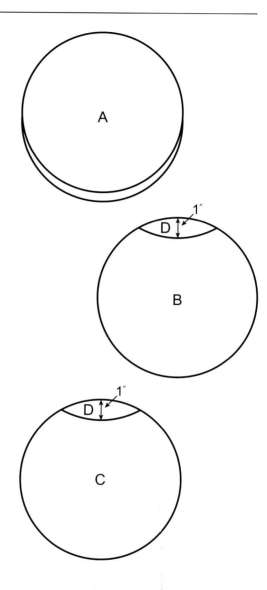

1. Tint coconut with green food coloring (see page 15 for directions).

2. Leave one cake layer whole; cut remaining two cakes as shown in illustration.

3. Using small amount of frosting to hold pieces together, arrange cake on serving tray as shown in photograph.

4. Frost cake with remaining frosting. Sprinkle with coconut.

5. Flatten gumdrops with rolling pin (see page 14 for directions); cut into shamrock shapes. Using decorating *icing,* outline the cake. Using decorating *gel,* outline gumdrop shamrocks and place on cake.

Makes 12 to 16 servings

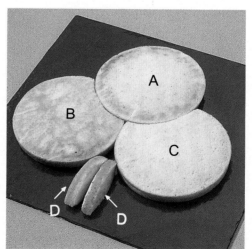

Old Glory

Serve this cake at any all-American get together.

2²/₃ cups BAKER'S ANGEL FLAKE Coconut, divided
Red food coloring
1 (13 × 9-inch) cake, cooled
1²/₃ cups Seven Minute Frosting (page 13) *or* thawed COOL WHIP Whipped Topping
1¹/₃ cups miniature marshmallows (for stripes)
Blue jelly beans (for stars)

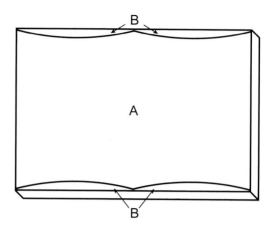

1. Toast ²/₃ cup of the coconut (see page 15 for directions); set aside. Tint remaining 2 cups coconut with red food coloring (see page 15 for directions).

2. Cut cake as shown in illustration.

3. Using small amount of frosting to hold pieces together, arrange cake on serving tray as shown in photograph.

4. Frost cake with remaining frosting. Sprinkle flag pole with toasted coconut. Alternate rows of red coconut and marshmallows to form stripes as shown in photograph. Use jelly beans for stars.

Makes 12 to 16 servings

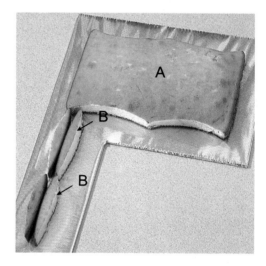

Firecrackers

Our firecracker cakes will put a bang into your Fourth of July barbecue. Each firecracker is generous enough to serve two.

5 cups BAKER'S ANGEL FLAKE Coconut
Red food coloring
24 cupcakes, cooled
5 cups Vanilla Buttercream Frosting (page 13)
Blue decorating gel (for piping stars)
Red sugar crystals (for garnish)
Blue sprinkles (for garnish)
Red string licorice (for fuses)

1. Tint coconut with red food coloring (see page 15 for directions).

2. Trim any "lips" off top edge of cupcakes.

3. Using small amount of frosting, attach bottoms of two cupcakes together as shown in photograph. Repeat with remaining cupcakes.

4. Stand attached cupcakes on one end on serving tray; frost. Pat coconut onto tops and sides.

5. Using decorating gel, draw a star on top of each firecracker. Sprinkle with red sugar crystals and blue sprinkles. Insert licorice for fuses.   *Makes 12 firecrackers*

Boo the Ghost

This adorable ghost has a creepy spider friend made out of licorice.

1 (13 × 9-inch) cake, cooled
2²/₃ cups Seven Minute Frosting (page 13) *or* **thawed COOL WHIP Whipped Topping**
2²/₃ cups BAKER'S ANGEL FLAKE Coconut
2 chocolate wafer cookies (for eyes)
2 green candy wafers (for eyes)
Candy corn (for mouth)
Black licorice sticks (cut to form spider's legs)
1 black jelly bean (for spider's body)

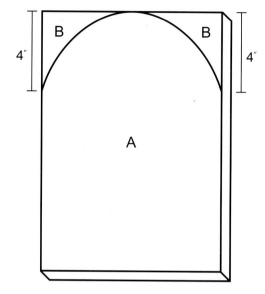

1. Cut cake as shown in illustration.

2. Using small amount of frosting to hold pieces together, arrange cake on serving tray as shown in photograph.

3. Frost cake with remaining frosting. Sprinkle with coconut.

4. Decorate cake as shown in photograph using remaining items listed in the ingredients.

Makes 12 to 16 servings

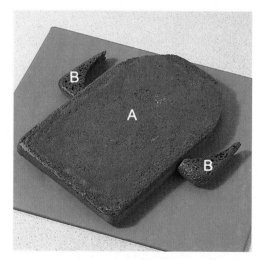

Whata Witch

1⅓ cups BAKER'S ANGEL
    FLAKE Coconut
  Red and yellow food
    colorings
 1 (9-inch) square cake, cooled*
2⅔ cups Vanilla Buttercream
    Frosting (page 13), divided
  Green food coloring
1⅓ cups Chocolate-Coated
    Coconut (page 15) (for hat)
 1 large black gumdrop (for eye)
 1 candy-coated chocolate
    candy (for eye)
  Red string licorice
    (for mouth)
 2 round candies (for warts)

Prepare and bake all of the cake batter in one (9-inch) square baking pan as directed in chart for selected recipe.

1. Tint coconut orange using red and yellow food colorings (see page 15 for directions).

2. Cut cake as shown in illustration.

3. Tint 1 cup of the frosting with green food coloring (see page 12 for directions).

4. Using small amount of plain frosting to hold pieces together, arrange cake on serving tray as shown in photograph.

5. Frost face of witch with green frosting. Frost witch's hat and hair with remaining plain frosting. Sprinkle witch's hat with Chocolate-Coated Coconut and witch's hair with orange coconut.

6. Flatten gumdrop with rolling pin (see page 14 for directions); cut into triangle for witch's eye. Decorate cake as shown in photograph using remaining items listed in the ingredients.

Makes 12 to 16 servings

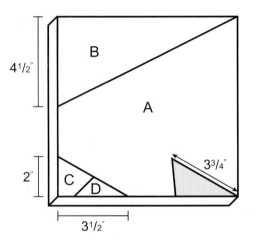

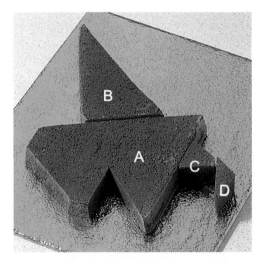

Pumpkin Patch Cake

Flattened black gumdrops (see page 14 for directions), cut into shapes, can turn this pumpkin cake into a festive Jack O' Lantern.

4 cups BAKER'S ANGEL FLAKE Coconut
Red and yellow food colorings
3½ cups Vanilla Buttercream Frosting (page 13), divided
Green food coloring
1 flat-bottomed ice cream cone (for stem)
2 cakes baked in 2 (12-cup) fluted tube pans, cooled*
1 cup Chocolate-Coated Coconut (page 15)

* Prepare and bake selected cake recipe two times using 12-cup fluted tube pan.

1. Tint coconut orange using red and yellow food colorings (see page 15 for directions).

2. Tint ½ cup of the frosting with green food coloring (see page 12 for directions). Frost outside of ice cream cone with about ¼ cup of the green frosting; set aside. Reserve remaining ¼ cup green frosting for piping lines on cake.

3. Using small amount of plain frosting to hold pieces together, stack two cakes, flat sides together, on serving tray as shown in photograph. (If desired, insert bamboo skewers into cake layers to hold the cakes together.)

4. Frost cakes with remaining plain frosting; sprinkle with orange coconut. Invert ice cream cone in hole on top to form "stem." Pipe reserved green frosting on pumpkin to form lines using a pastry bag fitted with a small plain tip. Arrange Chocolate-Coated Coconut around base of pumpkin to resemble dirt as shown in photograph.   *Makes 24 servings*

Turkey Gobbler

*When the gang's all in for the
holidays, serve this for dessert
as a nice change of pace from
pumpkin pie.*

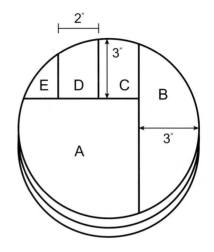

**2 (9-inch) round cake layers,
 cooled**
**4¼ cups Coconut Pecan Frosting
 (page 13)**
**11 small yellow gumdrops
 (for beak and garnish)**
**14 small red gumdrops
 (for garnish)**
**6 small orange gumdrops
 (for garnish)**
**1 round black licorice candy
 (for eye)**
**11 gumdrop orange slices
 (for tail feathers)**

1. Spread one cake layer with
1 cup of the frosting. Top with
remaining cake layer. Cut *layered*
cake as shown in illustration.

2. Using small amount of frosting
to hold pieces together,
arrange cake on serving tray as
shown in photograph.

3. Frost cake with remaining
frosting.

4. Flatten two yellow gumdrops
with rolling pin (see page 14
for directions); cut into triangles for
beak. Decorate cake as shown in
photograph using remaining items
listed in the ingredients.

Makes 12 to 16 servings

Snowman Cake

3½ cups Seven Minute Frosting
  (page 13) *or* thawed COOL
  WHIP Whipped Topping
1 cake baked in 1½-quart bowl,
  cooled*
1 cake baked in 1-quart bowl,
  cooled*
1 cake baked in 6-ounce
  custard cup, cooled*
4 round vanilla cookies
  (for hat brim)
1 red licorice stick (for arms)
1 black licorice stick (for arms)
2 cups BAKER'S ANGEL
  FLAKE Coconut
1½ cups Chocolate-Coated
  Coconut (page 15) (for hat)
1 large black gumdrop
  (for mouth)
2 miniature chocolate sandwich
  cookies (for eyes)
2 chocolate nonpareils
  (for eyes)
1 banana-shaped candy
  (for nose)
3 gumdrop rings (for buttons)
  Chewy fruit snack roll (cut
  into strips for scarf)

* Prepare selected cake recipe and bake as directed in chart in bowls indicated above.

1. Using small amount of frosting to hold pieces together, arrange cakes on serving tray, positioning large cake as body, medium cake as head and smallest cake as hat. Insert cookies into "seam" between head and hat to form brim of hat as shown in photograph.

2. Cut two ½-inch pieces from red licorice. Cut black licorice crosswise in half. Attach red licorice to black licorice with small amount of frosting to form stick arms; set aside.

3. Frost cookies and cake with remaining frosting. Sprinkle coconut over body and head of snowman. Cover hat and hat brim with Chocolate-Coated Coconut.

4. Flatten black gumdrop with rolling pin (see page 14 for directions); cut into long narrow strip to form snowman's mouth. Decorate cake as shown in photograph using gumdrop strip and remaining items listed in the ingredients.

Makes 12 to 16 servings

Rudy Reindeer

With his red nose so bright, Rudy is all ready to guide Santa's sleigh.

1 (13 × 9-inch) cake, cooled
2²/₃ cups BAKER'S ONE BOWL
    Chocolate Frosting
    (page 12)
2²/₃ cups Chocolate-Coated
    Coconut (page 15)
2 white candy wafers (for eyes)
2 round black candies
    (for eyeballs)
    Red licorice sticks
    (for antlers)
    Red and green chewy candies
    (for nose and garland)
    Green gumdrop spearmint
    leaves (for holly leaves)
    Red cinnamon candies
    (for holly berries)

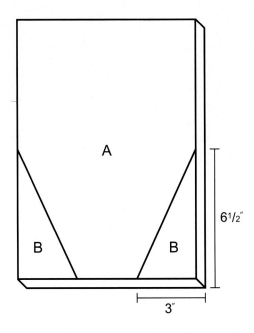

1. Cut cake as shown in illustration.

2. Using small amount of frosting to hold pieces together, arrange cake on serving tray as shown in photograph.

3. Frost cake with remaining frosting. Sprinkle with Chocolate-Coated Coconut. Decorate cake as shown in photograph using remaining items listed in the ingredients.

Makes 12 to 16 servings

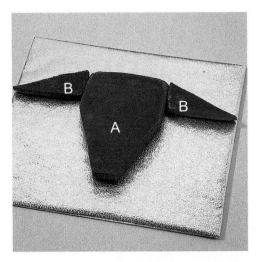

Buckaroo Bull: This cut-up shape can easily be made into a bull. In place of the candy decorations used for reindeer: bend one red licorice stick to form a nose ring, place two yellow chewy candies for nostrils, flatten two large red gumdrops for eyes and add two black chewy candies for eyeballs.

Jolly Santa

2½ cups BAKER'S ANGEL
        FLAKE Coconut, divided
    Red food coloring
  1 (8-inch) round cake layer,
        cooled
  1 (9-inch) square cake, cooled*
1²/₃ cups Seven Minute Frosting
        (page 13) *or* thawed COOL
        WHIP Whipped Topping
  8 large black gumdrops
        (for eyes, eyebrows, boots
        and belt)
  2 white jelly beans (for eyes)
  1 large red gumdrop (for nose)
    Red string licorice
        (for mouth)
  1 starlight mint
        (for pompom)
  4 yellow candy-coated licorice
        candies (for belt buckle)

** Divide batter evenly between
8-inch round and 9-inch square
baking pans. Bake as directed in
chart for selected cake recipe.*

1. Tint 1½ cups of the coconut
   with red food coloring (see
page 15 for directions).

2. Leave round cake whole; cut
   square cake as shown in
illustration.

3. Using small amount of frosting
   to hold pieces together,
arrange cake on serving tray as
shown in photograph.

4. Frost cake with remaining
   frosting. Sprinkle remaining 1
cup white coconut on Santa to form
beard and fur trim. Sprinkle jacket
and hat with red coconut.

5. To form eyes, cut one black
   gumdrop in half. Top each
gumdrop half with jelly bean; place
on cake. Flatten remaining black
gumdrops with rolling pin (see page

14 for directions); cut to form
eyebrows, boots and belt.

6. Decorate cake as shown in
   photograph using remaining
items listed in the ingredients.

Makes 12 servings

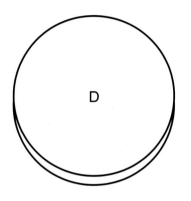

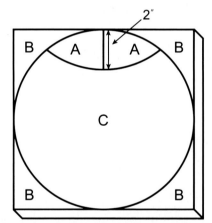

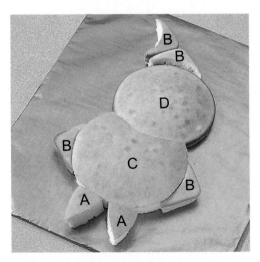

Merry Christmas Tree

The red candles on this creation can make it the perfect solution for a cake for a holiday birthday party.

2²/₃ cups BAKER'S ANGEL
        FLAKE Coconut, divided
    Green food coloring
  1 (9-inch) square cake, cooled*
2²/₃ cups Seven Minute Frosting
        (page 13) *or* thawed COOL
        WHIP Whipped Topping
    Large yellow gumdrop
        (for star)
    Red and white miniature jelly
        beans (for ornaments)
    Red string licorice
        (for garland)
    Red birthday candles
        (for tree lights), optional

* Prepare and bake all of the cake batter in one (9-inch) square baking pan as directed in chart for selected recipe.

1. Toast ¹/₃ cup of the coconut (see page 15 for directions). Tint remaining 2¹/₃ cups coconut with green food coloring (see page 15 for directions).

2. Cut cake as shown in illustration.

3. Using small amount of frosting to hold pieces together, arrange cake on serving tray as shown in photograph.

4. Frost cake with remaining frosting. Sprinkle trunk of tree with toasted coconut. Sprinkle tree with green coconut.

5. Flatten large yellow gumdrop with rolling pin (see page 14 for directions); cut into star shape with a small cookie cutter or sharp knife. Decorate cake as shown in photograph using remaining items listed in the ingredients.

Makes 12 to 16 servings

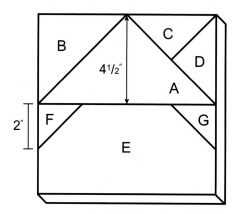

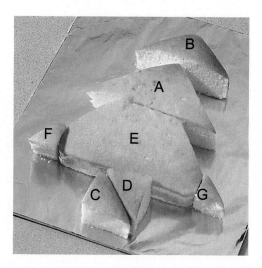

Mr. Rabbit

This friendly bunny is extra easy to make using two round cake pans.

2¼ cups BAKER'S ANGEL FLAKE Coconut, divided
Red food coloring
2 (9-inch) round cake layers, cooled
2⅔ cups Seven Minute Frosting (page 13) *or* thawed COOL WHIP Whipped Topping
2 green starlight mints (for eyes)
2 green gumdrops (for eyes)
Red string licorice (for whiskers and mouth)
1 small purple gumdrop (for nose)
Red licorice sticks (to outline bowtie)
Chewy candies (for bowtie)

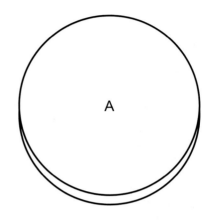

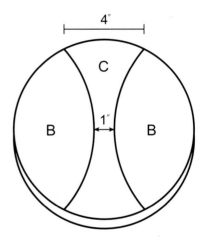

1. Tint ¼ cup of the coconut pink using red food coloring (see page 15 for directions).

2. Leave one cake whole; cut remaining cake as shown in illustration.

3. Using small amount of frosting to hold pieces together, arrange cake on serving tray as shown in photograph.

4. Frost cake with remaining frosting. Sprinkle center of bunny's ears with pink coconut. Sprinkle remaining 2 cups white coconut over bunny's head and outer edges of ears.

5. Decorate cake as shown in photograph using remaining items listed in the ingredients.

Makes 12 to 16 servings

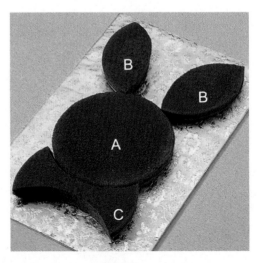

Ted E. Bear

3½ cups BAKER'S ANGEL
        FLAKE Coconut, divided
   1 (9-inch) round cake layer,
        cooled*
   1 (9-inch) square cake, cooled*
1½ cups BAKER'S ONE BOWL
        Chocolate Frosting
        (page 12)
  13 large marshmallows (for eyes
        and ends of paws)
   1 small red gumdrop
        (for mouth)
  12 black candy-coated licorice
        candies (for claws)
   2 green candy wafers (for eyes)
   3 chocolate-covered raisins
        (for eyes and belly button)
   1 malted milk ball (for nose)
     Red string licorice
        (for mouth)
   2 round chocolate cookies
        (for ears)

* Divide batter evenly between
9-inch round and 9-inch square
baking pans. Bake as directed in
chart for selected cake recipe.

1. Toast 2½ cups of the coconut
   (see page 15 for directions).

2. Leave round cake whole; cut
   square cake as shown in
illustration.

3. Using small amount of frosting
   to hold pieces together,
arrange cake on serving tray as
shown in photograph.

4. Frost cake with remaining
   frosting. Sprinkle remaining
1 cup white coconut on bear's
mouth and stomach. Sprinkle
toasted coconut on rest of bear.

5. Arrange three marshmallows
   at end of each paw. Cut

remaining marshmallow in half and
use for bear's eyes.

6. Flatten gumdrop slightly with
   rolling pin to form bear's
mouth. Decorate cake as shown in
photograph using remaining items
listed in the ingredients.

Makes 12 to 16 servings

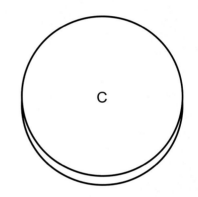

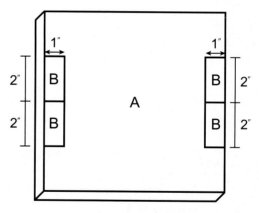

Cool Cat

This kitty's scarf is the cat's meow!

2 (9-inch) round cake layers,
    cooled
2 cups BAKER'S ONE BOWL
    Chocolate Frosting
    (page 12)
1½ cups BAKER'S ANGEL
    FLAKE Coconut
2 large green gumdrops
    (for eyes)
3 large black gumdrops
    (for whiskers)
½ red gumdrop ring (for mouth)
2 round black licorice candies
    (for eyes)
1 red jelly bean (for nose)
    Small gumdrops (for scarf)
1 large marshmallow (cut in
    half for paws)

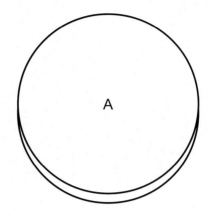

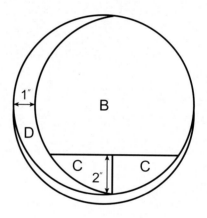

1. Leave one cake whole; cut remaining cake as shown in illustration.

2. Using small amount of frosting to hold pieces together, arrange cake on serving tray as shown in photograph.

3. Frost cake with remaining frosting. Sprinkle cat's chest, ears and tip of the tail with coconut.

4. Flatten large green and black gumdrops with rolling pin (see page 14 for directions); cut green gumdrops into eye shapes and cut black gumdrops into whiskers. Decorate cake as shown in photograph using remaining items listed in the ingredients.

Makes 12 to 16 servings

Caterpillar

This friendly creature can be as long or as short as your guest list. Just allow one cupcake for each guest.

3 cups BAKER'S ANGEL FLAKE Coconut
Green food coloring
3¹/₃ cups Seven Minute Frosting (page 13) *or* thawed COOL WHIP Whipped Topping
12 cupcakes, cooled
   Gumdrop orange slices (for feet)
   Black licorice sticks (cut to form antennae)
   Candy-coated licorice (for nose and spots)
2 candy-coated chocolate candies (for eyes)

1. Tint coconut with green food coloring (see page 15 for directions).

2. Arrange cupcakes on serving tray as shown in photograph. Frost tops and sides of cupcakes with frosting; press green coconut into frosting.

3. Decorate cake as shown in photograph using remaining items listed in the ingredients.

Makes 12 servings

Honey Bunny

Serve this yummy bunny at your next Easter get-together. It would also be great at a springtime tea. Kids will love to help.

2²/₃ cups BAKER'S ANGEL FLAKE Coconut, divided
Yellow and red food colorings
2 (9-inch) round cake layers, cooled
3 cups Seven Minute Frosting (page 13) *or* thawed COOL WHIP Whipped Topping
2 green jelly beans (for eyes)
Black licorice sticks (cut to form eyelashes and whiskers)
1 large marshmallow (for nose)
1 small red gumdrop (for nose)
Red string licorice (for mouth)

1. Tint 2¹/₃ cups of the coconut with yellow food coloring and tint remaining ¹/₃ cup coconut pink using red food coloring (see page 15 for directions).

2. Cut cakes as shown in illustrations.

3. Using small amount of frosting to hold pieces together, arrange cake on serving tray as shown in photograph.

4. Frost cake with remaining frosting. Sprinkle pink coconut to form bunny's cheeks, center of ears and paws. Sprinkle yellow coconut over bunny's head and body.

5. Decorate cake as shown in photograph using remaining items listed in the ingredients.

Makes 12 servings

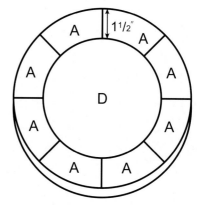

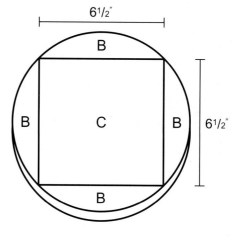

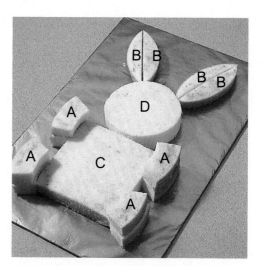

Ella Elephant

When the circus comes to town, you'll want to celebrate by serving this charming cake.

3½ cups **BAKER'S ANGEL FLAKE Coconut**
   Red food coloring
2 **(9-inch) round cake layers, cooled**
3 **cups Seven Minute Frosting (page 13) *or* thawed COOL WHIP Whipped Topping**
1 **marshmallow circus peanut (for end of elephant's trunk)**
   Red string licorice (for tail)
1 **disk-shaped candy (for eye)**
   Black licorice stick (cut to form eyelashes)
12 **miniature blue jelly beans (for toenails)**
1 **banana-shaped candy (for tusk)**
3 **chocolate wafer cookies (for ear)**

1. Tint coconut pink using red food coloring (see page 15 for directions).

2. Leave one cake whole; cut remaining cake as shown in illustration.

3. Using small amount of frosting to hold pieces together, arrange cake on serving tray as shown in photograph.

4. Frost cake with remaining frosting. Sprinkle with coconut.

5. Decorate cake as shown in photograph using remaining items listed in the ingredients.
   Makes 12 to 16 servings

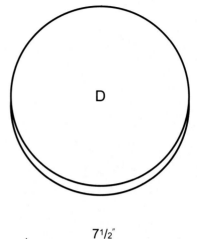

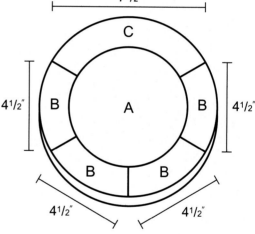

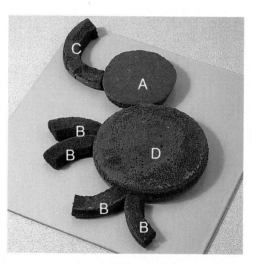

Dinosaur

This purple dinosaur is covered with assorted candies and is not the least bit scary.

4 cups Seven Minute Frosting (page 13) *or* **thawed COOL WHIP Whipped Topping**
Blue and red food colorings
1 (13 × 9-inch) cake, cooled
Assorted candies (for eyes and spots)
Candy-coated licorice candies (for mouth, back and toenails)

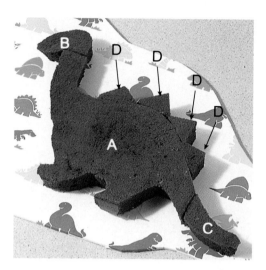

1. Tint frosting purple using blue and red food colorings (see page 12 for directions).

2. Cut cake as shown in illustration.

3. Using small amount of frosting to hold pieces together, arrange cake on serving tray as shown in photograph.

4. Frost cake with remaining frosting.

5. Decorate cake as shown in photograph using remaining items listed in the ingredients.

Makes 12 to 16 servings

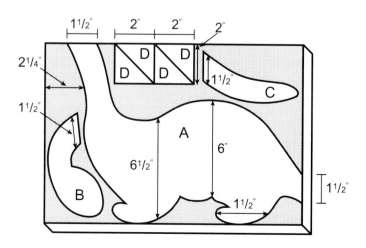

Wacky Quacky Duck

2²/₃ cups BAKER'S ANGEL
    FLAKE Coconut, divided
    Yellow and red food colorings
1 (9-inch) round cake layer,
    cooled*
1²/₃ cups Vanilla Buttercream
    Frosting (page 13)
    Chewy fruit snack roll
    (cut into strip for bow)
1 small purple gumdrop
    (for eye)
    Miniature flower candy
    (for bow decoration)

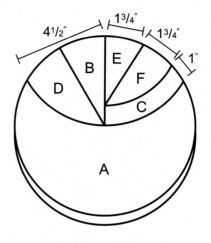

Prepare and bake selected cake recipe in two (9-inch) round baking pans. Use one layer for cake. Reserve remaining layer for another use.

1. Tint ²/₃ cup of the coconut with yellow food coloring and tint ¹/₃ cup of the remaining coconut orange using yellow and red food colorings (see page 15 for directions).

2. Cut cake as shown in illustration.

3. Using small amount of frosting to hold pieces together, arrange cake on serving tray as shown in photograph.

4. Frost cake with remaining frosting. Sprinkle feet and bill with orange coconut. Sprinkle wing with small amount of yellow coconut. Combine remaining yellow coconut with remaining 1²/₃ cups white coconut; sprinkle over body and head of duck.

5. Decorate cake as shown in photograph using remaining items listed in the ingredients.

Makes 6 servings

Mouse

6 cupcakes, cooled*
1 cake baked in 1½-quart bowl,
   cooled*
1⅔ cups Seven Minute Frosting
   (page 13) *or* thawed COOL
   WHIP Whipped Topping
2⅔ cups BAKER'S ANGEL
   FLAKE Coconut
2 round vanilla cookies
   (for ears on big mouse)
1 pink candy mint (for nose on
   big mouse)
2 large red gumdrops (for eyes
   on big mouse)
   Red string licorice
   (for whiskers, eyelashes
   and tails)
   Red cinnamon candies
   (for eyes and noses on
   baby mice)
   Candy wafers (for ears on
   baby mice)

*Prepare and bake selected cake
recipe as directed in chart in muffin
pan and bowl.*

1. Cut 1-inch cube from one of
the cupcakes as shown in
illustration. Set aside remaining
small pieces of cupcake for
snacking or other use.

2. Arrange cake pieces on
serving tray as shown in
photograph.

3. Using small amount of frosting,
attach cake cube to bottom
edge of bowl cake. Fill in gaps with
frosting to form a nose.

4. Frost cake and *tops only* of
remaining cupcakes with
remaining frosting. Sprinkle coconut
over frosting on cake and
cupcakes.

5. Decorate cake and cupcakes
as shown in photograph using
remaining items listed in the
ingredients.

Makes 12 to 16 servings

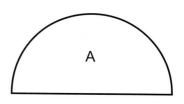

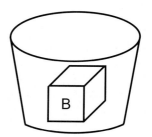

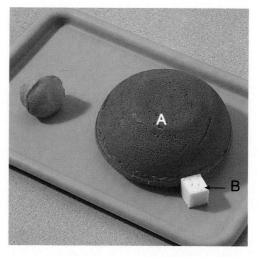

Flutters the Butterfly

Our pretty butterfly is a cheery yellow color. Decorate his wings with your favorite candies.

2 cups BAKER'S ANGEL FLAKE Coconut
Yellow food coloring
1 (13 × 9-inch) cake, cooled
4 cups Vanilla Buttercream Frosting (page 13)
Small red and green gumdrops (for body and wing decorations)
Licorice bites (cut in half for wing decorations)
Red string licorice (for antennae)

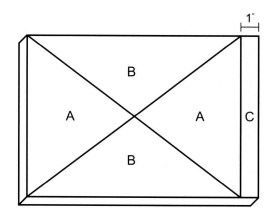

1. Tint coconut with yellow food coloring (see page 15 for directions).

2. Cut cake as shown in illustration.

3. Using small amount of frosting to hold pieces together, arrange cake on serving tray as shown in photograph.

4. Frost cake with remaining frosting. Sprinkle with coconut.

5. Flatten three red and seven green gumdrops with rolling pin (see page 14 for directions); cut into shapes for body and wing decorations. Decorate cake as shown in photograph using remaining items listed in the ingredients.

Makes 12 to 16 servings

Spot the Dog

This cake is perfect for dog lovers of all ages. It would be great to celebrate the arrival of a new puppy!

1 (13 × 9-inch) cake, cooled
2²/₃ cups Seven Minute Frosting (page 13) *or* thawed COOL WHIP Whipped Topping
4 gumballs (for collar)
  Chewy fruit snack roll (for collar)
2½ cups BAKER'S ANGEL FLAKE Coconut
1 cup Chocolate-Coated Coconut (page 15) (for ears, tail and spots)
1 small red gumdrop (for tongue)
  Red string licorice (for outlines and mouth)
2 round black licorice candies (for eye and nose)
  Black candy-coated licorice candies (for feet)

1. Cut cake as shown in illustration.

2. Using small amount of frosting to hold pieces together, arrange cake on serving tray as shown in photograph.

3. Attach gumballs to chewy fruit snack roll with small amount of frosting to form collar; set aside. Frost cake with remaining frosting. Place collar around neck of dog. Sprinkle cake with coconut. Place Chocolate-Coated Coconut on dog to form ears and spots.

4. Flatten gumdrop with rolling pin (see page 14 for directions); cut to form tongue. Decorate cake as shown in photograph using remaining items listed in the ingredients.

Makes 12 to 16 servings

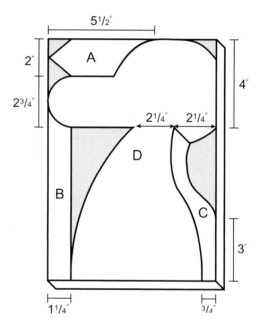

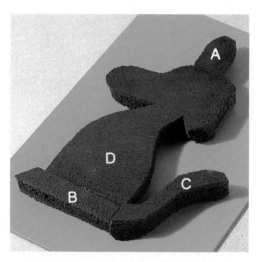

Pink Piggy

2½ cups BAKER'S ANGEL
   FLAKE Coconut
Red food coloring
1 cake baked in 6-ounce
   custard cup, cooled*
2 (9-inch) round cake layers,
   cooled*
2¼ cups Vanilla Buttercream
   Frosting (page 13)
2 large white gumdrops
   (for ears)
1 chocolate sandwich cookie,
   cut in half (for eyes)
1 pink jelly beans (cut in half
   for eyes)
12 red jelly beans (for toenails)
8 white jelly beans
   (for necklace)
2 black jelly beans (for nose)
Red string licorice
   (for eyelashes and tail)
1 red licorice stick (for mouth)

*Prepare and bake selected cake
recipe as directed in chart in one
(6-ounce) custard cup and two
(9-inch) round baking pans.*

1. Tint coconut pink using red
food coloring (see page 15 for
directions).

2. Leave custard cup cake and
one cake whole; cut remaining
cake as shown in illustration.

3. Using small amount of frosting
to hold pieces together,
arrange cake on serving tray as
shown in photograph.

4. Frost cake with remaining
frosting. Sprinkle cake with
pink coconut.

5. Flatten gumdrops with rolling
pin (see page 14 for directions);

cut and pinch into two ear shapes.
Decorate cake as shown in
photograph using remaining items
listed in the ingredients.

Makes 12 to 16 servings

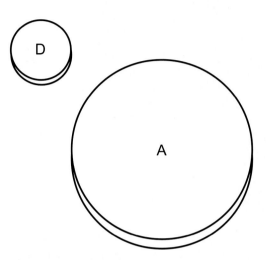

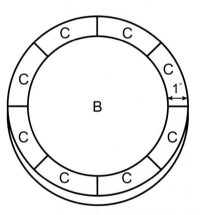

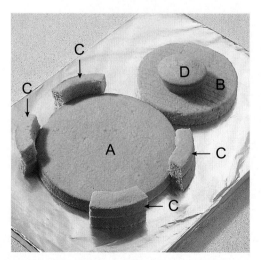

Play Ball

1⅓ cups BAKER'S ANGEL
        FLAKE Coconut
    Red food coloring
1 (8-inch) round cake layer,
        cooled*
1 cake baked in 6-ounce
        custard cup, cooled*
1 cake baked in 1½-quart bowl,
        cooled*
1 cup BAKER'S ONE BOWL
        Chocolate Frosting
        (page 12)
1½ cups Chocolate-Coated
        Coconut (page 15)
    Red string licorice (for cap
        seams and for lacing on
        ball and glove)
1½ cups Vanilla Buttercream
        Frosting (page 13)
1 red candy-coated chocolate
        candy (for button on cap)
2 large black gumdrops
        (for cap emblems)

*Prepare and bake selected cake
recipe as directed in chart in pan
and bowls as indicated above.*

1. Tint coconut with red food
coloring (see page 15 for
directions).

2. Cut 8-inch cake as shown in
illustration A.

3. Using small amount of
chocolate frosting to hold
pieces together, arrange cake for
glove on serving tray as shown in
photograph.

4. Frost glove with remaining
chocolate frosting. Sprinkle
with Chocolate-Coated Coconut.
Decorate with red string licorice as
shown in photograph.

5. Frost custard cup cake with
¼ cup of the vanilla frosting.
Decorate with red string licorice as

shown in photograph. Place
baseball on glove as shown in
photograph.

6. Cut cake baked in bowl as
shown in illustration. Using
small amount of frosting to hold
pieces together, arrange cake on
serving tray as shown in
photograph.

7. Frost cap with remaining vanilla
frosting. Decorate with red
string licorice and red candy as
shown in photograph. Sprinkle with
red coconut. Flatten gumdrops with
rolling pin (see page 14 for
directions); cut into emblem shapes
and place on cap as shown in
photograph.

Makes 12 to 16 servings

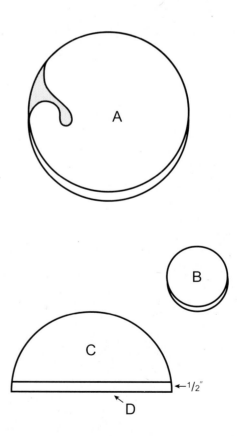

Rollin' Fun

Have your friends skate on over for a piece of this eye-catching cake.

**2²/₃ cups BAKER'S ANGEL
    FLAKE Coconut, divided
    Blue, yellow, green and red
    food colorings
1 (13×9-inch) cake, cooled
2 round chocolate-frosted
    creme-filled snack cakes** *or*
    **miniature chocolate
    doughnuts (cut in half
    horizontally for wheels)
2 cups Vanilla Buttercream
    Frosting (page 13)
    Red string licorice (for laces)
    Black licorice bites
        (for buckles)**

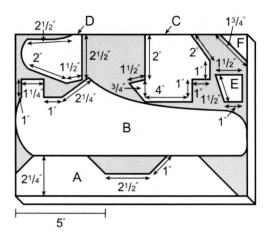

1. Tint 2 cups of the coconut with blue food coloring, tint ¹/₃ cup of the remaining coconut bright yellow using yellow and green food colorings and tint remaining ¹/₃ cup coconut pink using red food coloring (see page 15 for directions).

2. Cut cake as shown in illustration.

3. Using small amount of frosting to hold pieces together, arrange cake on serving tray as shown in photograph.

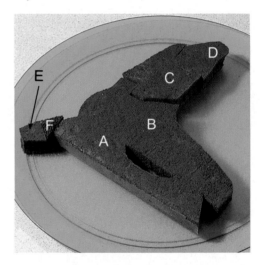

4. Frost cake with remaining frosting. Attach snack cake halves to form wheels.

5. Sprinkle cake with different colors of coconut as shown in photograph. Decorate cake as shown in photograph using remaining items listed in the ingredients.

Makes 12 to 16 servings

Football

When it's time for dessert or a treat in front of the TV on game day, the gang will all huddle around this cake.

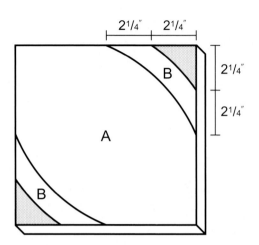

1 (9-inch) square cake, cooled*
2 cups BAKER'S ONE BOWL Chocolate Frosting (page 12)
1½ cups Chocolate-Coated Coconut (page 15)
23 miniature marshmallows (for bands)
Red string licorice (for lacings)

* Prepare and bake all of the cake batter in one (9-inch) square baking pan as directed in chart for selected recipe.

1. Cut cake as shown in illustration.

2. Using small amount of frosting to hold pieces together, arrange cake on serving tray as shown in photograph.

3. Frost cake with remaining frosting, filling in gaps with frosting. Sprinkle cake with Chocolate-Coated Coconut.

4. Decorate cake as shown in photograph using remaining items listed in the ingredients.

Makes 12 to 16 servings

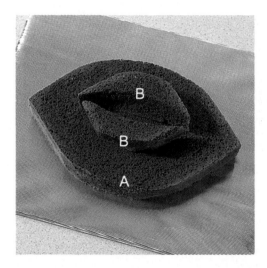

Tennis Racket

Have a U.S. Open or Wimbledon party and serve an ace with this tennis racket.

1½ cups BAKER'S ANGEL FLAKE Coconut, divided
Yellow and green food colorings
1 (13 × 9-inch) cake, cooled
2 cups Vanilla Buttercream Frosting (page 13)
Red string licorice (for ball)
Candy-coated chocolate candies (for grip)
Colored sprinkles (for handle and base of racket)
Green decorating gel (for strings)

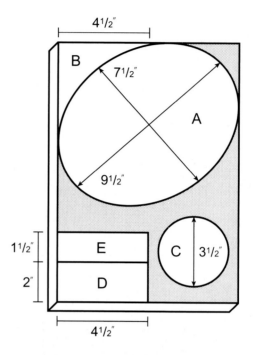

1. Toast 1¼ cups of the coconut (see page 15 for directions). Tint remaining ¼ cup coconut bright yellow using yellow and green food colorings (see page 15 for directions).

2. Cut cake as shown in illustration.

3. Using small amount of frosting to hold pieces together, arrange cake on serving tray as shown in photograph.

4. Frost racket and ball with remaining frosting. Sprinkle ball with bright yellow coconut. Decorate ball with licorice as shown in photograph.

5. Sprinkle toasted coconut on sides of racket. Pipe strings with decorating gel. Decorate cake as shown in photograph using remaining items listed in ingredients.

Makes 12 to 16 servings

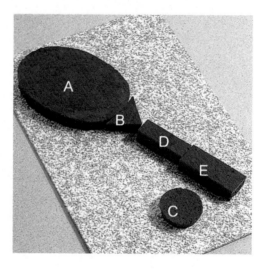

Sailboat

Ship ahoy! There's smooth sailing ahead with this colorful sailboat.

1 (9-inch) square cake, cooled*
1²/₃ cups Vanilla Buttercream Frosting (page 13)
1 cup Chocolate-Coated Coconut (page 15) (for hull)
Chocolate decorating icing *or* licorice stick (for mast)
1 large yellow gumdrop (for star)
1 large green gumdrop (for anchor)
4 round candies with holes (for portholes)

*Prepare and bake all of the cake batter in one (9-inch) square baking pan as directed in chart for selected recipe.

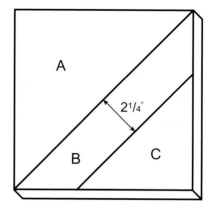

1. Cut cake as shown in illustration.

2. Using small amount of frosting to hold pieces together, arrange cake on serving tray as shown in photograph.

3. Frost cake with remaining frosting. Sprinkle hull of boat with Chocolate-Coated Coconut. Using decorating icing, pipe a mast on the boat.

4. Flatten gumdrops with rolling pin (see page 14 for directions); cut yellow gumdrop in the shape of a star and cut green gumdrop in the shape of an anchor. Decorate cake as shown in the photograph using remaining items listed in the ingredients.

Makes 12 to 16 servings

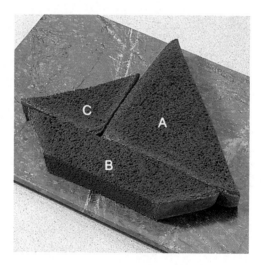

Hobby Horse

This polka dot hobby horse will win everyone's heart. BAKER'S ONE BOWL Chocolate Cake (page 10) with Chocolate Frosting (page 12) makes him the perfect cake for chocolate lovers.

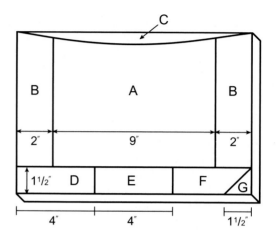

1 (13 × 9-inch) cake, cooled
3¹/₃ cups BAKER'S ONE BOWL Chocolate Frosting (page 12)
2 cups BAKER'S ANGEL FLAKE Coconut
Large gumdrops (for polka dots)
Chocolate-covered mint patties (for polka dots)
Candy-coated chocolate candies (for saddle)
Red licorice stick (for tail)
1 round black licorice candy (for eye)
Red string licorice (for harness and reins)

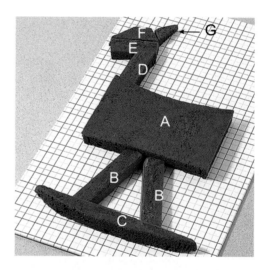

1. Cut cake as shown in illustration.

2. Using small amount of frosting to hold pieces together, arrange cake on serving tray as shown in photograph.

3. Cut gumdrops in half; press slightly to flatten. Attach to chocolate-covered mint patties with small amount of frosting to form polka dots; set aside.

4. Frost cake with remaining frosting. Use candy-coated chocolate candies to outline saddle as shown in photograph. Sprinkle coconut over entire cake *except* for saddle and rocker.

5. Decorate cake as shown in photograph using remaining items listed in the ingredients.

Makes 12 to 16 servings

Rag Doll

1²/₃ cups BAKER'S ANGEL
    FLAKE Coconut, divided
  Red, yellow and blue food
    colorings
  1 (8-inch) round cake layer,
    cooled*
  1 (8-inch) square cake, cooled*
2¹/₃ cups Vanilla Buttercream
    Frosting (page 13)
  2 large black gumdrops
    (for shoes)
  2 large red gumdrops (for nose,
    mouth and heart)
  Black licorice sticks (cut to
    form mouth, eye lashes and
    eyebrows)
  2 green candy wafers (for eyes)
  2 black round hard candies
    (for eyes)
  Red licorice stick (for collar
    decoration)
  1 multi-colored candy (for neck
    decoration)
  Red string licorice
    (for stockings)
  Candy-coated chocolate
    candies (for dress and shoe
    buttons)

*Divide batter evenly between
8-inch round and 8-inch square
baking pans. Bake as directed in
chart for selected cake recipe.*

1. Tint ²/₃ cup of the coconut
orange using red and yellow
food colorings and tint ²/₃ cup of the
remaining coconut with blue food
coloring (see page 15 for
directions).

2. Cut cakes as shown in
illustrations.

3. Using small amount of frosting
to hold pieces together,
arrange cake on serving tray as
shown in photograph.

4. Frost cake with remaining
frosting. Sprinkle orange
coconut on top and sides of head
for hair. Sprinkle blue and
remaining ¹/₃ cup white coconut for
dress and pinafore.

5. Flatten black and red
gumdrops with rolling pin (see
page 14 for directions); cut out
shoes, nose, mouth and heart.
Decorate cake as shown in
photograph using remaining items
listed in the ingredients.

Makes 12 to 16 servings

Note: To make a boy rag doll, use
the "C" pieces cut from the square
cake for the doll legs in place of the
"A" pieces cut from the round cake.
Frost and decorate as desired.

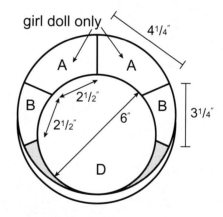

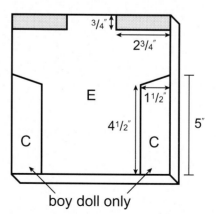

Happy Clown

1 cup BAKER'S ANGEL FLAKE
  Coconut, divided
  Green, red and yellow food
  colorings
1 (8-inch) round cake layer,
  cooled*
1 (8-inch) square cake, cooled*
2²/₃ cups Vanilla Buttercream
  Frosting (page 13)
1 red licorice stick (for hat
  band)
2 chocolate wafer cookies
  (for eyes)
2 vanilla wafer cookies
  (for eyes)
1 red round hard candy
  (for nose)
  Red string licorice
  (for mouth)
1 green gumdrop ring
  (for bowtie)
1 small orange gumdrop
  (for bowtie)
  Gumballs or round hard
  candies (for bowtie)
  Colored sugar crystals
  (for bowtie)

*Divide batter evenly between
8-inch round and 8-inch square
baking pans. Bake as directed in
chart for selected cake recipe.*

1. Tint ½ cup of the coconut with green food coloring and tint remaining ½ cup coconut orange using red and yellow food colorings (see page 15 for directions).

2. Cut cakes as shown in illustrations.

3. Using small amount of frosting to hold pieces together, arrange cake on serving tray as shown in photograph.

4. Frost cake with remaining frosting. Sprinkle green

coconut on hat and orange coconut around top and sides of head for hair.

5. Decorate cake as shown in photograph using remaining items listed in the ingredients.

Makes 12 to 16 servings

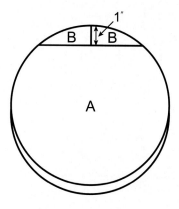

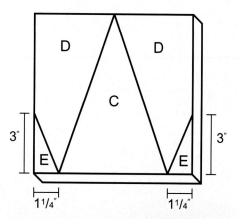

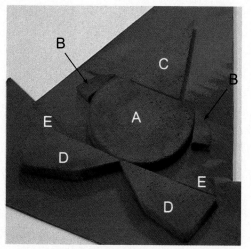

Choochoo Train

This train cake will be the perfect centerpiece for your child's birthday party. For an added treat, load each car with a cargo of candy on top of the coconut.

**2 cups BAKER'S ANGEL
    FLAKE Coconut, divided
Assorted food colorings
1 (13 × 9-inch) cake, cooled
3⅓ cups Vanilla Buttercream
    Frosting (page 13)
Assorted square candies
    (for engine windows)
Red string licorice
    (for engine)
2 green starlight mints
    (for engine)
1 banana-shaped candy
    (for engine)
1 green gumdrop (for engine)
Red licorice sticks (for car
    connectors)
2 chocolate sandwich cookies
    (for rear engine wheels)
30 miniature chocolate sandwich
    cookies (for all other
    wheels)
34 candy-coated chocolate
    candies (for wheels and
    headlights)
16 miniature bear-shaped
    cookies (for train
    passengers)**

1. Divide coconut into four ½-cup portions. Tint each portion of the coconut a different color (see page 15 for directions).

2. Cut cake as shown in illustration.

3. Use small amount of frosting, attach smaller cake pieces to the top of one of the larger pieces for the engine. Arrange cake pieces on serving tray as shown in photograph.

4. Frost sides and top of engine. Generously sprinkle coconut of desired color over top of engine. Decorate engine as shown in photograph.

5. Frost sides and tops of cars. Generously sprinkle colored coconut on top of each car. Attach cars to each other with licorice sticks, cut into pieces.

6. For wheels, use frosting to attach candy-coated chocolate candies to cookies. Press bear-shaped cookies onto sides of cars and front engine.

Makes 16 servings

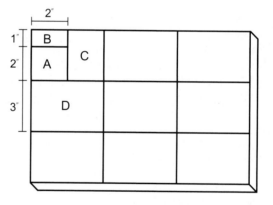

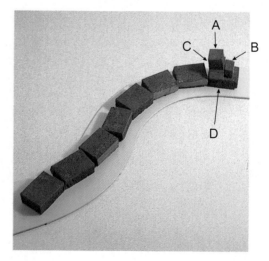

Bearplane

A bon voyage party would be incomplete without an airplane cake or serve it at your aspiring top gun's birthday party.

2 cups BAKER'S ANGEL FLAKE Coconut, divided
Yellow and blue food colorings
1 (13 × 9-inch) cake, cooled
3½ cups Vanilla Buttercream Frosting (page 13)
Candy-coated chocolate candies (for windows)
Chewy candies (for lights)
Blue decorating gel (for tailpiece strips)
1 miniature bear-shaped cookie (for pilot)

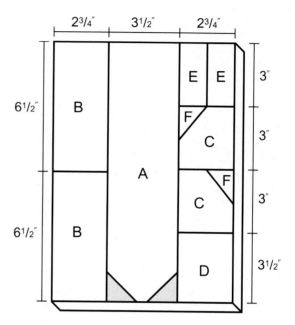

1. Tint ¼ cup of the coconut with yellow food coloring and tint ¼ cup of the remaining coconut with blue food coloring (see page 15 for directions).

2. Cut cake as shown in illustration.

3. Using small amount of frosting to hold pieces together, arrange cake on serving tray as shown in photograph.

4. Frost cake with remaining frosting. Sprinkle with remaining 1½ cups white coconut and yellow and blue coconuts as shown in photograph.

5. Decorate cake as shown in photograph using remaining items listed in the ingredients.

Makes 12 to 16 servings

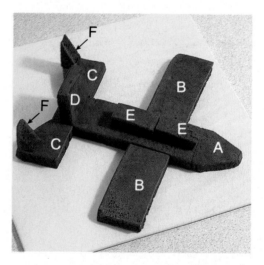

Monster Truck

2²/₃ cups Vanilla Buttercream
　　　Frosting (page 13)
Blue food coloring
2 (9 × 5-inch) loaf cakes,
　　　cooled*
1 cup BAKER'S ONE BOWL
　　　Chocolate Frosting
　　　(page 12)
5 large doughnuts (for wheels)
8 small gumdrops (for lights
　　　and hubcaps)
8 candy-coated licorice candies
　　　(for trim)
2 red starlight mints
　　　(for headlights)
　Red licorice sticks (for trim)
　Red string licorice
　　　(for wipers)

** Prepare and bake selected cake
recipe as directed in chart in two
(9 × 5-inch) loaf pans.*

1. Tint 1⅓ cups of the vanilla
frosting with blue food coloring
(see page 12 for directions).

2. Leave one cake whole; cut
remaining cake as shown in
illustration.

3. Using small amount of plain
frosting to hold pieces
together, arrange cake on serving
tray as shown in photograph. Insert
bamboo skewers into cake pieces
to hold in place, if necessary.

4. Reserve a small amount of
chocolate frosting to attach
wheels to truck. Frost base and
1 inch of bottom of truck with
remaining chocolate frosting. Frost
windows with plain frosting. Frost
roof and body of truck with blue
frosting.

5. Secure doughnut wheels and
gumdrop hubcaps to base of
truck with reserved chocolate
frosting. Decorate cake as shown in
photograph using remaining items
listed in ingredients. Remove
skewers before serving.

Makes 12 to 16 servings

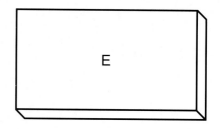

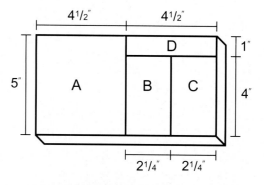

Space Shuttle

Your party will really take off with this cake as the main attraction.

**1½ cups BAKER'S ANGEL
    FLAKE Coconut, divided
Red and blue food colorings
1 (13 × 9-inch) cake, cooled
2¼ cups Vanilla Buttercream
    Frosting (page 13)
Blue decorating icing
    (for lettering)
Blue jelly beans (for garnish)
Red licorice sticks (for outline
    and exhaust)**

1. Tint ½ cup of the coconut with red food coloring and tint remaining 1 cup coconut with blue food coloring (see page 15 for directions).

2. Cut cake as shown in illustration.

3. Using small amount of frosting to hold pieces together, arrange cake on serving tray as shown in photograph.

4. Frost cake with remaining frosting. Sprinkle red coconut over tip of shuttle to form space shuttle's nose. Sprinkle blue coconut over wings.

5. Using decorating icing, write "U.S.A." on body of shuttle. Decorate cake as shown in photograph using remaining items listed in the ingredients.

Makes 12 to 16 servings

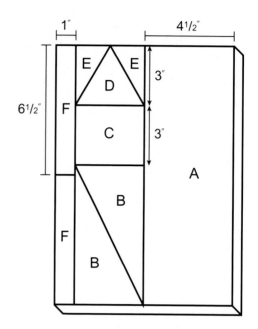

Cowboy Boot

Hey pardner — serve this cake at the next round-up.

1 (13 × 9-inch) cake, cooled
2 cups Vanilla Buttercream Frosting (page 13)
1 cup BAKER'S ONE BOWL Chocolate Frosting (page 12)
1 large green gumdrop (for cactus)
14 round candy disks (for spur chain)
12 large candy-coated licorice candies (for boot's trim)
½ gumdrop ring (for boot's loop)
Silver dragées *or* small candies (for boot and spur decoration)

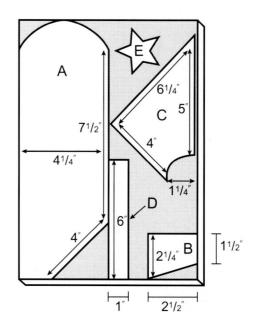

1. Cut cake as shown in illustration.

2. Using small amount of vanilla frosting to hold pieces together, arrange cake on serving tray as shown in photograph.

3. Frost heel and sole of boot with chocolate frosting. Frost boot with remaining vanilla frosting.

4. Flatten large green gumdrop with rolling pin (see page 14 for directions); cut into cactus shape. Decorate cake as shown in photograph using remaining items listed in the ingredients.

Makes 12 to 16 servings

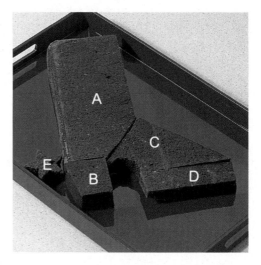

Daisy

Please do eat the daisy!

5⅓ cups BAKER'S ANGEL
　　FLAKE Coconut, divided
　Green and yellow food
　　colorings
　2 (9-inch) round cake layers,
　　cooled
　3 cups Vanilla Buttercream
　　Frosting (page 13)
　9 small red gumdrops
　　(for flower center)
　9 round pink mints
　　(for flower center)

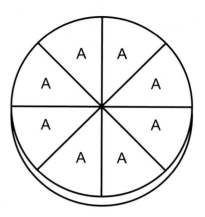

1. Tint 2⅓ cups of the coconut with green food coloring and tint ⅓ cup of the remaining coconut with yellow food coloring (see page 15 for directions).

2. Cut cakes as shown in illustrations.

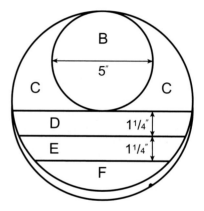

3. Using small amount of frosting to hold pieces together, arrange cake on serving tray as shown in photograph.

4. Frost cake using remaining frosting. Sprinkle green coconut on stem. Sprinkle yellow coconut over center of flower. Sprinkle petals with remaining 2⅔ cups white coconut. Decorate cake as shown in photograph using remaining items listed in the ingredients.

Makes 12 to 16 servings

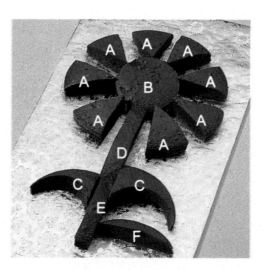

Baby Booties

These little baby bootie cakes are almost as precious as the eagerly awaited bundle of joy.

4 cups Seven Minute Frosting (page 13) *or* **thawed COOL WHIP Whipped Topping, divided**
Assorted food colorings
24 cupcakes, cooled
2 cups BAKER'S ANGEL FLAKE Coconut
Decorating icing (for shoelaces)
Miniature star candies (for garnish)

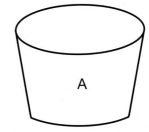

1. Divide frosting into four 1-cup portions. Tint each portion of the frosting a different color (see page 12 for directions).

2. Leave sixteen cupcakes whole; cut remaining cupcakes as shown in illustration.

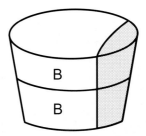

3. Using small amount of frosting to hold pieces together, assemble booties on serving tray as shown in photograph.

4. Frost four booties with each color of frosting; sprinkle with coconut.

5. Pipe decorating icing on the booties to form shoelaces.

6. Decorate booties as shown in photograph using miniature star candies.

Makes 16 servings

Umbrella

This umbrella is perfect for celebrating the impending arrival of a baby. For a wedding shower, tint the coconut the colors of your party decorations.

**2½ cups BAKER'S ANGEL FLAKE Coconut, divided
Assorted food colorings
1 (13 × 9-inch) cake, cooled
4 cups Vanilla Buttercream Frosting (page 13)
½ cup small white jelly beans**

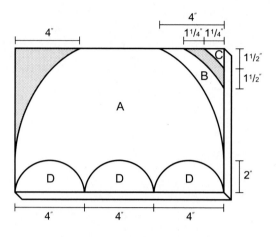

1. Toast ¼ cup of the coconut (see page 15 for directions). Divide remaining coconut into three (¾-cup) portions. Tint each portion of the coconut a different color (see page 15 for directions).

2. Cut cake as shown in illustration. Split *each* half circle horizontally in half to make six half circles.

3. Using small amount of frosting to hold pieces together, arrange cake on serving tray as shown in photograph.

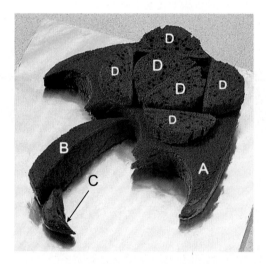

4. Frost umbrella and handle with remaining frosting.

5. Sprinkle top of handle with toasted coconut. Sprinkle colored coconuts as shown in photograph. Arrange jelly beans to outline three sections of the umbrella.

Makes 12 to 16 servings

PARTY TIPS

- Use a cut-up cake to create a theme for a party.

- Determine when your party is to be and for what event. Sports events and holidays are popular times to have parties.

- Invite your guests 10 to 14 days in advance of the party.

- On a sheet of paper, write down the names of the people invited and check them off as they accept or decline.

- Write your menu down with references where the recipes are found (cookbook, recipe box, etc.).

- Make a list of all the foods and beverages you will need. Buy whatever you can ahead of time.

- Determine how much time each item takes to prepare and make each as far ahead as possible (like make the cake!).

- Make festive trays from large items found around the house—just cover them with foil and paper doilies or wrapping paper for a festive look.

- Do the simple chores a day before. Set up the serving bowls, glasses and utensils. Decorate the house.

- Try to allow at least 30 minutes for relaxing before the start of the party.